GEOGRAPHY   Y6 / P7

GW01564173

Teacher's Notes
Mountains

Andrew Hammond

Series editor | Sue Palmer

Contents

OXFORD
UNIVERSITY PRESS

OXFORD
UNIVERSITY PRESS

Great Clarendon Street, Oxford OX2 6DP

Oxford University Press is a department of the University of Oxford.
It furthers the University's objective of excellence in research, scholarship,
and education by publishing worldwide in

Oxford New York

Auckland Bangkok Buenos Aires Cape Town Chennai
Dar es Salaam Delhi Hong Kong Istanbul Karachi Kolkata
Kuala Lumpur Madrid Melbourne Mexico City Mumbai Nairobi
São Paulo Shanghai Taipei Tokyo Toronto

Oxford is a registered trade mark of Oxford University Press
in the UK and in certain other countries

British Library Cataloguing in Publication Data

Data available

ISBN 978 0 19 834877 1

19 18 17 16 15 14 13 12 11

Typeset by Fakenham Photosetting, Fakenham, Norfolk

Printed in the UK

Paper used in the production of this book is a natural, recyclable product
made from wood grown in sustainable forests. The manufacturing process
conforms to the environmental regulations of the country of origin.

What is Oxford Connections?

Oxford Connections is a set of 12 cross-curricular books and related teaching materials for 7 to 11 year olds. The books will help you teach literacy through a science, geography or history-based topic. Each book provides the material to cover one unit from the QCA Schemes of Work for the National Curriculum in England and Wales, and the non-fiction literacy objectives for one whole year of the National Literacy Strategy. (You can find a grid of where the QCA and NLS objectives are covered on p 48 of these notes and on the inside back cover of the pupils' books.) The books can be used to focus primarily on literacy or on science/geography/history.

Literacy

Pupils need different literacies. As well as traditional texts with different purposes and audiences, they also need to be able to understand and write material presented in different forms such as diagrams, bullet points, notes and Internet displays, particularly when working with non-fiction.

Oxford Connections supports the development of these different literacies. It focuses particularly on reading and writing non-fiction, and will help pupils use effectively the different non-fiction text types (report, explanation, instructions, recount, discussion, persuasion).

Using these books will help pupils to focus on the two main elements which make a text type what it is:

◆ The language features used (for example, present tense for instructions, and past tense for recounts, use of commands in instructions).

◆ The structure of the text (for example, chronological order, in the case of instructions or recounts).

The structure of a text can be represented as a diagram or framework, showing visually how the parts of the text fit together, which are the main points and how they are developed. (A very common example of this type of presentation is a timeline, which shows events which have happened in the past, as a continuum, the order of which cannot change.) In these notes, we refer to material presented in this diagrammatic way as *visual* (*visual reports, visual explanations,* etc.).

Pupils will learn to read and to present information visually (by using frameworks), thus developing good note-taking skills, and consolidating their understanding of how texts are structured. The visual texts, in particular, are accessible to those pupils who need more support. Using frameworks to plan their own writing will also help to improve all pupils' planning and drafting/editing skills.

In these notes, we have used icons to represent the different sorts of frameworks you can use, called *skeletons.* These are referred to in the *National Literacy Strategy Support Materials for Text Level Objectives* (DfES 0532/2001). They can be used as an aide-memoire to help pupils remember the structure of each text type. They appear on pp 6–47 to show you what text types are on the pupils' book pages.

Recount	┤┤┼→	Explanation	O→O→O
Instructions	O→O→O→	Persuasion	✳⟨ ✳⟨ ✳⟨
Non-chronological report		Discussion	

Using *Mountains* to teach literacy

There are step-by-step instructions to teach pupils how to read and write the different text types on pages 18–47 (a six-page section for each text type). They follow this model:

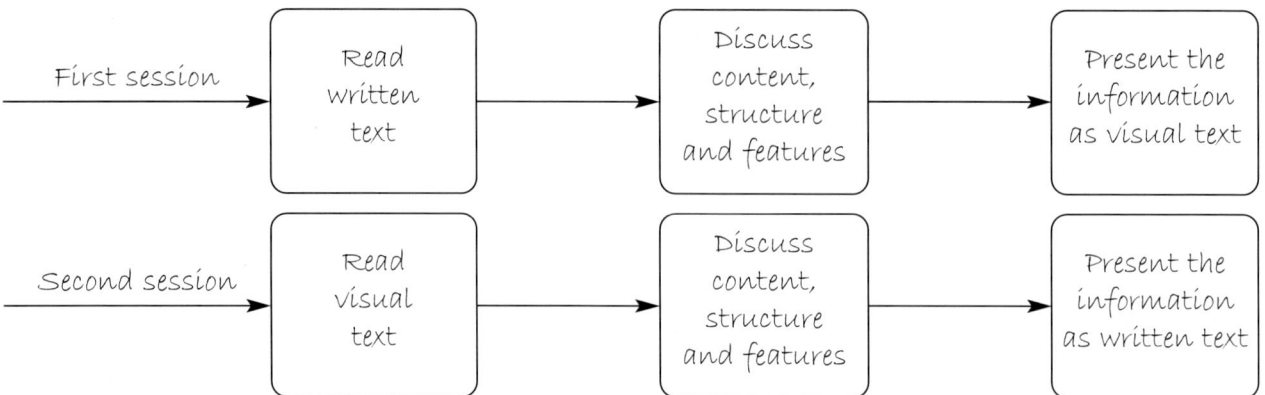

Each six-page section contains:

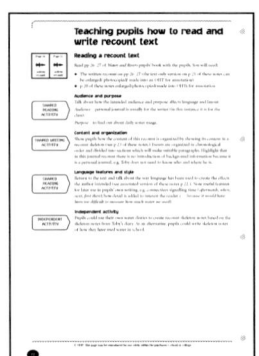 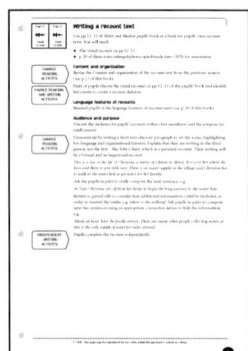

Two pages of step-by-step instructions taking you through the process described in the diagram above. They will help you analyse a written text, and then produce a visual version of that text with a group of pupils. You will then analyse a visual text, producing a written version.

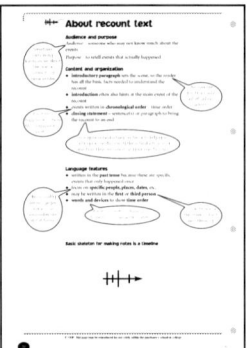

A page describing the relevant text type*

An example of the text type (an excerpt from *Mountains*) for you to read and analyse with pupils*

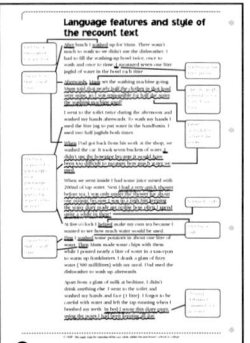

The same example with language features highlighted for your reference*

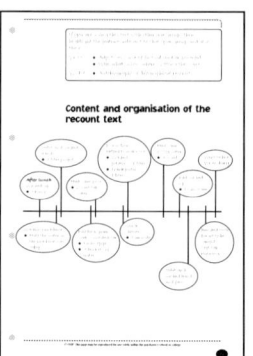

A visual version of the written text for your reference*

these can be photocopied as handouts, a poster or an OHT

There are page-by-page notes on how to use the material kto cover other aspects of literacy on pp 6–17. These page-by-page notes also show how to use the material in the pupils' book for the particular subject, e.g. geography.

Speaking and listening, and drama

The discussion which is inherent in this method of learning should improve pupils' speaking and listening skills. As well as helping pupils to organize and structure their ideas before writing, visual texts should prompt pupils to use the relevant language features orally, as well as in writing. Additional speaking and listening, and drama activities such as those below, can be used to further reinforce the pupils' learning.

Retelling – events can be retold by an individual or by groups taking a section from a visual recount

Role-play – using the visuals created by the whole class to ask/answer questions in role as the person in the recount or as someone taking one side of the argument.

Mini plays – retelling an event or following an explanation visual to show how something works. Pupils could be the different parts of whatever is being explained.

Puppet plays – retelling an event or following an explanation visual

Freeze-frame – pupils in groups could show sections from a recount visual or report visual. They could show different aspects of a discussion.

TV/radio reports – demonstrating knowledge using a visual report as a TV/radio report. In a TV report images could be used either pictorially or by the use of freeze-framing.

TV demonstrations – following an instruction visual or explanation visual to demonstrate making something or explaining how something works.

TV/radio interviews – retelling events in recounts or using report visuals while interviewing another pupil/pupils in role.

TV/radio adverts – using a persuasive visual to make adverts.

Illustrated talks – using the visual as a prompt.

Hot seat – answering questions in role – either as a persuasion, report or recount.

Debates – using discussion visuals to have debates between individuals or groups.

Using *Mountains* to teach Geography

Mountains contains all the material you need to cover this topic, and to achieve the objectives of the *QCA Scheme of Work for the National Curriculum Geography Unit 15* (recommended for Year 6 pupils). There are page-by-page notes on how to use the material for geography on pp 6–17. You can find a grid showing how the QCA objectives are covered on p 48 of these notes, and on the inside back cover of *Mountains* pupils' book.

Which year group should I use *Mountains* with?

Mountains has been written for Year 6 pupils (10–11 year olds). However, if your school places the topic in another year group, the geography material contained in *Mountains* will still be suitable for use with other age groups. Although all of the non-fiction literacy objectives for Year 6 are covered, many of the objectives for other year groups are also supported. Most of the six non-fiction text types are covered in it, and language features for Years 3, 4 and 5 are highlighted in the relevant sections.

NB Throughout this introduction the term Year 6 has been used to mean 10–11 year olds. The references in the grid on p 48 are to the *National Literacy Strategy* and to the *QCA Scheme of Work for the National Curriculum*. However, *Mountains* is suitable for use with P7 in Scotland and in Northern Ireland, since it supports many elements of the *National Guidelines, 5–14* and *The Northern Ireland Curriculum*. The geography content of *Mountains* does not conflict in any way with either *National Guidelines, 5–14* or *The Northern Ireland Curriculum*.

> SCOTLAND
> AND NORTHERN
> IRELAND

Geography

Use these pages as advance organizers to provide pupils with an overview of the work to be carried out:

concept map shows the main areas to be covered and links between them.

contents page shows how information has been organized in the book.

- Use the quotation as an aide for using the contents page – ask pupils to find what is being mentioned.
- Return to the pages occasionally during teaching to help pupils see how their learning and understanding is developing.
- Use these pages as a revision aid, asking pupils to summarize what they know about each aspect.
- Use the concept map at the end of the topic to review all areas of the topic covered.

Literacy

- Establish the links between the concept map and the contents page. Look at similarities and differences between them. (e.g. they contain the same information but organized differently; the concept map provides an overview of the ideas in the book, the contents page provides an ordered guide to what the book contains).
- Let pupils practise finding information using the contents page and index until they are confident enough to find requested information quickly.

Geography

Key concepts

- To learn about different types of environments and specifically a mountain one.
- To learn about the world distribution of major mountain areas.
- To use globes and atlases.
- To learn how the environment affects the nature of human activity.

Key vocabulary

- *deserts, mountains, oceans, forests – broadleaf, coniferous, rain*

Suggested activities

- Ask the pupils to locate the places mentioned on a globe or in an atlas. Ask pupils to name and locate other oceans and name and locate other desert areas.
- Ask the pupils to prepare two-minute presentations using cue cards, in pairs or individually, on a specific location. In each case, whether they choose a mountain, desert or forest, the pupils must investigate evidence of human settlements, wildlife, plants and climate.

Literacy

Page 4	Page 5
visual report	visual report

- For the presentation mentioned in the 'suggested activities' above, the pupils will need to first of all write a written report and then transfer their evidence onto cue cards for the purposes of presenting it to the class.
- Ask the pupils to write a piece of descriptive prose describing their chosen location (from the above exercise). To prepare for this task, choose one of the landscapes and encourage the pupils to imagine they are in that place. Ask them to use all their senses to think of powerful figurative language associated with such an environment. Collect any adjectives, nouns, similes and metaphors on the board in a spidergram.
- Ask the pupils to write descriptive poems inspired by each location.

Geography

Key concepts

◆ To learn about different types of environments and specifically a mountain one.
◆ To learn about the world distribution of major mountain areas.
◆ To use globes and atlases.
◆ To learn how the environment affects the nature of human activity.

Key vocabulary

◆ *tribes, ethnic groups, Sherpas, high altitude, Mount Kinabalu, Andes, Incas*

Suggested activities

◆ Investigate the effects high altitude has on temperature and air quality. Ask the pupils to research why the air is thinner on mountain tops than in the valleys below. Notice how Sherpa climbers can climb without extra oxygen supply while other visiting climbers need to carry tanks and masks. (Link to Science)
◆ Research the Andes mountain range – find out which seven countries it spans and investigate the range of settlements, old and new, which can be found there.

Literacy

Page 6	Page 7
written report	written report

These pages are used as a featured example to teach the reading and writing of **report** text (see pp 30–35 of these teacher's notes).

Also use to:

◆ Ask the pupils to research and write up a report on the Incas. Gather together photographs of famous Inca sites from travel brochures and discuss the importance they hold for tourists today and for the tourist industry in the area.

Geography

Key concepts

◆ To learn about different types of environments and specifically a mountain one.
◆ To learn about the world distribution of major mountain areas.
◆ To use globes and atlases.
◆ To learn how the environment affects the nature of human activity.

Key vocabulary

◆ *mountain range, peak*

Suggested activities

◆ Use the recorded lengths and heights of the mountains to practise converting kilometres to meters. Rewrite each total length in meters and each highest peak in kilometres. (Link to Maths)
◆ Construct a line graph or block chart to show the recorded lengths and heights of the mountain ranges. This can also be done using a computer program. Use as a classroom display showing the relative sizes and lengths of the ranges. (Link to Maths and ICT)
◆ Using atlases and maps, locate a mountain range. Look in finer detail at the landscape and water sources. Link closely with a study of keys and symbols in map work.

Literacy

Page 8	Page 9
visual report	visual report

◆ Identify the features of a report (see p 32 of these notes).
◆ Use the notes from the page and information gleaned from the world map to make report skeletons for some of the mountain ranges or peaks.
◆ Pupils use the skeletons to write up short written reports on the mountains and mountain ranges.

Pages 10–11

Geography

Key concepts
- To learn about different types of environments and specifically a mountain one.
- To learn about the world distribution of major mountain areas.
- To use globes and atlases.
- To learn how the environment affects the nature of human activity.

Key vocabulary
- *headwaters, condense, glaciers, food supply, fauna, flora*

Suggested activities
- Ask the pupils to use maps to find a mountain range in the UK and to trace the rivers and streams running off it. See if they can locate the watershed (see the Glossary).
- Discuss the water cycle. Draw a diagram illustrating how it works and the role mountains play in this process.
- Bring into class a selection of tea and coffee packets and find out where the tea and coffee is grown; locate on a world map. *Are they grown in upland areas*?
- Research on the Internet what is being done to protect endangered species and find out more about the ones mentioned. (Link to ICT)

Literacy

Page 10	Page 11
written explanation	written explanation

- In groups, pupils prepare notes using an explanation skeleton (see p 38 of these notes). They then use the notes to prepare a presentation to the rest of the class clearly explaining why mountains are so important.
- Ask the pupils to research the fauna and flora of a specific mountain, using a range of secondary sources and then write up their evidence in a non-chronological written report.

Pages 12–13

Geography

Key concepts
- To investigate how mountain environments are similar and different in nature across a range of places and scales.
- To use secondary sources.

Key vocabulary
- *glaciers, wadis, peaks, climate, subtropical, inhabited*

Suggested activities
- Using the information and photographs, pupils compare and contrast the mountain ranges, looking specifically at habitation, climate, appearance and height.
- Ask the pupils to find out more about the Grampian Mountains in Scotland, e.g. location, fauna and flora, population, rivers, lochs, canals, transport links, climate, nearest cities/towns.

Literacy

Page 12	Page 13
visual report	visual report

- Discuss the features of the visual report (see p 32 of these notes) – noting in particular the following:
  - separate boxes
  - photographs
  - bulleted points
  - concise phrases
  - limited description (mostly factual).

- The information on the mountains of Sinai provides an example of a written report. Ask the pupils to rewrite this text box in skeleton form and then in precise factual form, using bullets.
- Pupils choose one or more of the bulleted boxes to write up as written reports, first compiling a skeleton of the information to help plan paragraphs.
- Pupils combine their work to create a tourist brochure aimed at people interested in climbing and walking in the mountains.

Geography

Key concepts
◆ To investigate how mountain environments are similar and different in nature across a range of places and scales.
◆ To use secondary sources.

Key vocabulary
◆ *fold, fault, dome, volcano, erosion, Earth's crust, plates*

Suggested activities
◆ Ask the pupils to use a range of secondary sources to locate examples of each type of mountain formation around the world.
◆ Find out more about volcanoes – there is a wealth of books and Internet websites on this subject. Ask the pupils to show the location of a number of volcanoes on a map of the world. (Link to ICT)
◆ Find evidence of cases where volcanic eruptions have in the past had a devastating effect on local settlements and wildlife, e.g. Pompeii. (Link to History)

Literacy

Page 14	Page 15
◌→◌→◌	◌→◌→◌
written explanation	visual explanation

These pages are used as a featured example to teach the reading and writing of **explanation** text (see pp 36–41 of these teacher's notes).

Also use to:
◆ Ask pupils to write poems based on an eruption following on from their research and work on volcanoes. Encourage the pupils to use personification and other imagery to portray the volcano as a dark, forbidding giant, sleeping for now, but with the potential to cause destruction at any time.
◆ Write short playscripts set on a volcanic island – in which the villagers hear news that the volcano, dormant for years, is about to erupt again.

Geography

Key concepts
◆ To investigate how mountain environments are similar and different in nature across a range of places and scales.
◆ To use secondary sources.

Key vocabulary
◆ *volcanic activity, steam, ash, minerals, magma, lava, vulcanologists, evacuation, eruption, ashfall*

Suggested activities
◆ Conduct further research into a particular volcano. Look at how the natural resources it provides are gathered or farmed. Also investigate the lives of the local inhabitants – how do they depend upon the volcano for resources and/or tourism? When was the last time the local town had to be evacuated? Discuss the photograph of Popocatepetl erupting.
◆ Ask the pupils to take it in turns to assume the role of a local resident of a volcanic island and to answer questions from the class (or in pairs) on how the volcano impacts upon their life. (Link to Drama)
◆ Pupils design and construct three-dimensional 'working' models of volcanoes. (Link with Art, Design and Technology)

Literacy

Page 16	Page 17
◌→◌→◌	◌→◌→◌
written explanation	visual instruction

Page 16
◆ Pupils write notes using a flowchart (see p 41 of these notes). Point out how the headings and subheadings will help.

Page 17
◆ Ask pupils to rewrite the instructions as written instructions. Make reference to the following features of instruction text: title tells what is to be done; list of items required; diagram(s); sequenced steps; use of imperative verbs; factual descriptions.

Pages 18–19

Geography

Key concepts
◆ To learn about weather patterns in different parts of the world.
◆ To learn that varying weather conditions can have a significant impact upon life in an area.
◆ To use secondary sources.

Key vocabulary
◆ *mountain climate, peak, higher and lower slopes*

Suggested activities
◆ Discuss the different habitats provided at different heights. Ask pupils to find more examples of animals and birds that live on the lower slopes of the mountains.
◆ What characteristics do the animals living on the higher slopes have in common? (Link to Science)
◆ Discuss which animals live in mountain areas in the UK. Have any pupils been to upland areas in this country or other countries? What do they remember about the vegetation? Why does vegetation become less the further up the mountain?
◆ Choose a specific mountain (e.g. Mount Kilimanjaro), and find out more details about its flora, fauna and weather conditions.

Literacy

Page 18	Page 19
⚛	⚛
visual report	visual report

◆ Ask the pupils to rewrite the visual report as a written report. Remind pupils of the features of report text (see p 32 of these notes). Also note the use of paragraphs to separate the information for peak, higher and lower slopes.
◆ Pupils make notes first in the form of a report skeleton.

Pages 20–21 & 22

Geography

Key concepts
◆ To learn about weather patterns in different parts of the world.
◆ To learn that varying weather conditions can have a significant impact upon life in an area.
◆ To use secondary sources.

Key vocabulary
◆ *blizzard, snowdrift, survival techniques, avalanche, hypothermia, evacuated*

Suggested activities
◆ After carrying out further research into the hazards of becoming stranded at high altitude, ask the pupils to assume the role of the skiers. In groups, the pupils prepare and perform three scenes: inside the 'marmot's den'; the rescue; a press interview. (Link to Drama)
◆ Find out and discuss what causes an avalanche and where in the world they are most common. Using secondary sources – find out about any recent avalanches that may have happened. (Link to ICT)
◆ Pupils use atlases to find the Kumaon Hills and the Kali river. Discuss reasons for the landslide.
◆ Discuss how climate plays an important part in the disasters. In pairs, pupils discuss and write down ideas for preventing these disasters happening again.

Literacy

Page 20	Page 21	Page 22
⊬⊢⊢→	⊬⊢⊢→	⊬⊢⊢→
written recount	written recount	written recount
⊬⊢⊢→	⊬⊢⊢→	
visual recount	visual recount	

Pages 20–21
These pages are used as a featured example to teach the reading and writing of **journalistic recount** text (see pp 24–29 of these notes).

Also use to:
◆ Ask pupils to write up the events in diary form, as though written by one of the skiers. Note features of diary writing: personal responses and reactions; chronological; references to time, day, weather, temperature.

Page 22

◆ Ask the pupils to write a newspaper recount based on the events in the diary.

◆ Invite pupils to assume the roles of guests at the hotel discussing the recent avalanche. Or television news correspondents, sent to the town to report on the tragic events. (Link to Drama)

Page 23

Geography

Key concepts

◆ To learn about weather patterns in different parts of the world.

◆ To learn that varying weather conditions can have a significant impact upon life in an area.

◆ To use secondary sources.

Key vocabulary

◆ *temperature, rainfall, Celsius, millimetre*

Suggested activities

◆ Discuss the charts. Ask the pupils to work out the difference between summer temperatures in the Andes and in the Alps and then winter temperatures between the two mountains. (Link to Maths)

◆ Discuss the best time of year to go to the mountain ranges, depending on the purpose, e.g. *What time of year is it best to go climbing in the Himalayas?*

◆ Ask the pupils to find climate data for other mountain ranges (use books, atlases and websites). Pupils present the data in graphs. (Link to Maths)

Literacy

Page 23
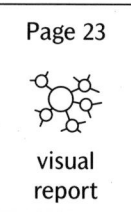
visual report

◆ Pupils use the rainfall charts to write a written report in the style of the report for temperature. Use a report skeleton to order information.

◆ Pupils write a report for a holiday brochure, describing the weather conditions in either the Himalayas, Alps or Andes.

Pages 24–25

Geography

Key concepts

◆ To learn about different types of environment and specifically a mountain one.

◆ To learn how the environment affects the nature of human activity.

Key vocabulary

◆ *traditional farming and crafts, mining, energy production, forestry, tourism, mountain climate*

Suggested activities

◆ Discuss how mountain areas support a range of different industries and how these industries depend upon the climate associated with mountains.

◆ Discuss how important these industries are in sustaining a mountain's population.

◆ Each of the industries featured could be researched further. (Link to ICT)

◆ Look more closely at the forestry industry – find out the route logs take from being felled to finishing up as paper and wood products.

◆ Point out how sudden changes in climate (blizzards, heavy rainfall, avalanches) can have a very damaging effect on local industries.

Literacy

Page 24	Page 25
visual report	visual report

These pages are used as a featured example to teach the reading and writing of **report** text (see pp 30–35 of these teacher's notes).

Also use to:

◆ Ask the pupils to choose a specific industry, for example, rice farming, and write a non-chronological report. (More data and written evidence can be found in a range of secondary sources.)

Geography

Key concept
◆ To learn how the environment affects the nature of human activity.

Key vocabulary
◆ *conservationists, renewable resource, logging, endangered animals*

Suggested activities
◆ The topic of deforestation is a contentious one and there is a plethora of material available from books, magazines, atlases and Internet websites. Ask pupils to focus on one rainforest region or forested area and carry out research into the programme of clearing and re-planting trees.

◆ Find out other animals/birds that are threatened by extinction because of forest clearance. Make a classroom display, showing where in the world these creatures live and information about them. Describe how their habitat is being changed. (Link with Science)

Literacy

Page 26	Page 27
written discussion	written discussion

These pages are used as a featured example to teach the reading and writing of **discussion** text (see pp 42–47 of these teacher's notes).

Also use to:
◆ Ask the pupils to prepare persuasive speeches for a class debate using the following motion:

This House believes that the rainforests of the world should be left untouched by humans, native population excepted.

When writing the persuasive speeches, pupils should be mindful of the following features: a sentence or paragraph to **introduce the argument**; followed by the **main points,** each of which may need some **elaboration**; and finally a **concluding sentence or paragraph** to sum up the argument.

Geography

Key concept
◆ To learn how the environment affects the nature of human activity.

Key vocabulary
◆ *tourism, outdoor pursuits, remote, cut off, avalanches*

Suggested activities
◆ In pairs, the pupils assume the roles of two villagers, one who enjoys living in the mountain resort, and the other who only sees the disadvantages. Ask the pupils to plan, rehearse and perform a two-minute conversation between the villagers. (Link to Drama)

◆ Use as the basis of a class discussion on the effects of tourism in mountain regions. Try to encourage the pupils to see both sides of the issues and to recognize that whilst tourism can generate revenue, it can also be an intrusion into the daily lives of the locals (read in conjunction with pp 40–41 of the pupils' book).

Literacy

Page 28	Page 29
visual discussion	visual discussion

These pages are used as a featured example to teach the reading and writing of **discussion** text (see pp 42–47 of these teacher's notes).

Also use to:
◆ Ask the pupils to imagine they are a local child, living in a popular mountain holiday resort. Ask them to prepare excerpts from a diary, chronicling the first few days of the holiday season and then the days after the tourists have left. Encourage the pupils to describe the feelings the child might experience, e.g. frustration, boredom, excitement, etc.

Pages 30–31

Geography

Key concept

◆ To learn how the environment affects the nature of human activity.

Key vocabulary

◆ *Charmonix, Mont Blanc, panoramic views, nature reserve, transportation, accommodation, itineraries*

Suggested activities

◆ Use as the basis of a discussion and study of Alpine ski resorts in summer. Encourage the pupils to recognize the vast change in landscape and views during the summer months and investigate ways in which local tourist boards can attract visitors after the snow has gone.

◆ Locate Chamonix on a map. List the ways that visitors might reach the mountains. *Where is the nearest airport? Is there a motorway nearby?*

◆ Locate the different places that the Three Peaks Explorer holiday tour goes to on a map. Work out the total distance that the coach travels. (Link to Maths)

◆ Discuss who might be attracted to such a holiday and what they might like doing.

◆ Discuss reasons why it is important that these mountain areas encourage tourism.

Literacy

Page 30	Page 31
✳ ⋛ ✳ ⋛ ✳ ⋛ written persuasion	✳ ⋛ ✳ ⋛ ✳ ⋛ visual persuasion

Page 30

◆ Pupils make notes on the main points of the text using a persuasion skeleton.

Page 31

◆ Pupils write a persuasion text for a travel brochure using the notes and photographs.

◆ Ask the pupils to bring in a range of different travel brochures and use them to demonstrate style and content in preparation for writing the travel article.

Pages 32–33

Geography

Key concept

◆ To learn how the environment affects the nature of human activity.

Key vocabulary

◆ *Bedouin, charity, sponsor*

Suggested activities

◆ Ask pupils to research the location of Suilven and Mount Sinai using atlases.

◆ Ask pupils to compare the different climates the three writers of the postcards might be experiencing. *Why is it hot on Mount Sinai in January? Would it be so easy to climb Suilven in December?*

◆ Using the written descriptions, pupils draw/paint what they think the picture on the other side of the postcard is like. Discuss paint effects and colour to recreate the atmosphere. (Link to Art)

Literacy

Page 32	Page 33
⊢⊣⊢➤ written recount	✳ ⋛ ✳ ⋛ ✳ ⋛ written persuasion
⬡ written report	

◆ Ask pupils to write a timeline of the day's events described on the postcard from Sinai.

◆ Make notes on the information about Suilven using a report skeleton. Use the notes to write a more formal style report for a guide book of the area.

◆ Ask pupils to make notes in a pronged persuasion skeleton of the letter. Use the notes to design a poster on behalf of the Leprosy Mission, outlining the Mission's aim and giving details of the sponsored walk.

◆ Ask pupils to assume the role of Uncle Freddy or Aunty Eloise and write a reply, thanking Jonathan for writing and agreeing to sponsor him. Remind pupils to check the way their letter is laid out.

Pages 34–35

Geography

Key concept
◆ To learn how the environment affects the nature of human activity.

Key vocabulary
◆ *expeditions, dry cold, wet cold, survival*

Suggested activities
◆ Discuss why it is important to wear the right clothing and take the correct equipment when trekking or climbing in cold climates. (Link with Science)
◆ Ask pupils to research the type of foods that would be suitable to take and then compile a shopping list. Emphasize the importance of taking food that provides adequate nutrition. (Link with ICT and Science)
◆ In groups, ask pupils to consider and note down the highs and lows of being on an expedition in a cold and wet climate. They could list them in a table and then compare results with other groups. (Link to PSHE)
◆ Looking at a map of Britain, pupils decide on areas of the country that might be popular places to go trekking and climbing and then explain why.

Literacy

Page 34	Page 35
O→O→O→	O→O→O→
written instruction	written instruction

◆ Discuss with the pupils the key features of instruction text, e.g. imperative tense, chronological order, use of numbers or bullet points.
◆ Make notes on the text using a flowchart. Then use the notes as the basis for an eye-catching, informative poster to be displayed in a Youth Hostel, reminding climbers and walkers of the importance of wearing and taking the correct equipment.

Pages 36–37

Geography

Key concepts
◆ To learn about different types of environment and specifically a mountain one.
◆ To use secondary sources.

Key vocabulary
◆ *Edmund Hillary, Tenzing Norgay, summit, Everest*

Suggested activities
◆ Using a range of secondary sources, the pupils can research Hillary's expedition in 1953. Ask them, in particular, to answer two questions: *Why did they choose to climb in May and not in any other month? Why did they climb a particular route up the mountain?*
◆ Use as the basis for a class discussion on ambition. Hillary wished to become a climber and explorer from an early age – do any of the pupils have similar ambitions? Which frontiers will provide similar challenges when they are older? Space? Oceans? Deep inside the Earth? (Link to PSHE and Science)
◆ Discuss other places in the world that have offered a challenge to humans, e.g. North and South Pole, other mountains. Talk about how the weather always plays an important role in the success or failure of these attempts.

Literacy

Page 36	Page 37
⊢⊢↦	⊢⊢↦
visual recount	visual recount

These pages are used as a featured example to teach the reading and writing of **recount** text (see pp 18–23 of these teacher's notes).

Also use to:
◆ Write fictional diary excerpts based on this or any other famous expedition which the pupils have researched.

Geography

Key concepts
◆ To learn about different types of environment and specifically a mountain one.
◆ To use secondary sources.

Key vocabulary
◆ *mountains, glaciers, plateaux, Sir Edmund Hillary, George Mallory, Andrew Irvine*

Suggested activities
◆ Ask the pupils, in pairs, to prepare role-play scenes in which they play Hillary and Tenzing or Mallory and Irvine, as they approach the summit. Encourage the pupils to conduct accurate research first – so as to present a 'realistic' account of the ascent to the summit and the climatic conditions. (Link to Drama)
◆ Continue the role-play theme and invite pupils to join in a 'hot-seating' activity in which they field questions from the class in the role of one of the explorers – Noel Odell would be an interesting character to portray.

Literacy

Page 38	Page 39
written discussion	written recount

Page 38
◆ The question-and-answer material on this page could be used in a speaking and listening activity. (Link to Drama)
◆ Ask the pupils to write a similar interview script, this time interviewing Tenzing Norgay.

Page 39
This page is used as a featured example to teach the reading and writing of **recount** (biography) text (see pp 18–23 of these teacher's notes).

◆ When studying the biography of Mallory, remind the pupils of the importance of distinguishing between biographical and autobiographical text, including:
 – recognizing the distinction between first and third person and noticing the effect each narrative voice has on the reader
 – distinguishing between fact, opinion and fiction.

Geography

Key concepts
◆ To learn that the effect of tourism can be significant in a given area and can be both good and bad.
◆ To use secondary sources.

Key vocabulary
◆ *tourism, income, employment, environment, communities, extinction, landslides*

Suggested activities
◆ Initiate a lively class debate in which different members of the local community come together to share views on the wave of tourism which is hitting their town. Give out role-cards which provide the pupils with an occupation and a particular view, (examples might be, shopkeepers, hoteliers, council officials versus environmentalists, local historians, residents and commuters). (Link with Drama)

Literacy

Page 40	Page 41
visual discussion	visual discussion

◆ Ask the pupils to order the points in a discussion skeleton then use this as the basis for compiling an article for a Sunday newspaper. When writing the discussion/journalistic article, pupils should:
 – summarize fairly the competing views
 – analyze the strengths and weaknesses of different positions
 – try to remain impartial.
◆ Ask the pupils to write formal debate speeches in favour of or opposing the motion:

This House believes that tourism is destroying our town.

Pages 42–43

Geography

Key concept
◆ To learn that the effect of tourism can be significant in a given area and can be both good and bad.

Key vocabulary
◆ *conserve, respect, environment*

Suggested activities
◆ Prompt a discussion on the importance of observing the country code and respecting the environment in which we live.
◆ Ask the pupils to design posters encouraging visitors to respect their surroundings. Pupils consider where their posters might be best displayed and to also think about the readership. (Link to Art, Design and Technology)
◆ Discuss the knock-on effect of carrying out one of the anti-social activities illustrated, e.g. fire or polluting a stream. What animals/ birds are affected and habitats put at risk. (Link to Science)

Literacy

Page 42	Page 43
*≶ *≶ *≶ visual persuasion	*≶ *≶ *≶ visual persuasion

◆ Ask pupils to make notes using a pronged persuasion skeleton and then to use this as the basis for writing a persuasive leaflet for a bed and breakfast or hotel in a rural area.
◆ Ask the pupils to write a letter of complaint from a local resident to their MP, about the lack of respect for the environment shown by tourists and asking for action to be taken to avoid such behaviour in the future.
◆ Remind pupils that a cohesive argument is constructed through:
  – the expression, sequence and linking of points;
  – the provision of persuasive examples (litter/fire, etc.)
  – appealing to the known audience (i.e. fellow residents).

Pages 44–45

Geography

Key concepts
◆ To learn that the effect of tourism can be significant in a given area and can be both good and bad.
◆ To use secondary sources.

Key vocabulary
◆ *mountain environment*

Suggested activities
◆ Find out more about the environmental disasters mentioned in the headlines. Use books, magazines, newspapers and Internet websites. (Link to ICT)
◆ Ask the pupils to prepare (individually or in pairs) a class presentation on one of the headlines.

Literacy

Page 44	Page 45
∗ ∗*∗ *∗* visual discussion	*∗* ∗*∗ *∗* visual discussion

◆ Following on from their research, pupils complete the report to accompany the heading, writing it in journalistic style. And/or they could present the information as written discussion text.
◆ Use the headlines as a basis of a concluding essay (report/persuasion/discussion text) entitled 'It's Our Future', in which the pupils consolidate what they have learnt about environmental issues and share with the reader their own thoughts and hopes for the future. Their work should include:
  – an introduction – outlining the theme/viewpoint
  – a discussion of a number of examples where the environment is threatened
  – a comment upon global responsibility
  – mention of any positive steps already in place to save endangered regions/lives
  – conclusion – giving personal opinion and a vision for the future.

Pages 46

Geography

Key concept
◆ To learn about different types of environment and specifically a mountain one.

Suggested activity
◆ Use these pages to search for the meanings of key vocabulary to further the pupils' understanding of different aspects of mountains. Identify words from reading that are unknown and use the glossary to further understanding and to clarify information learnt.

Literacy

Use these pages to demonstrate how to locate information confidently and efficiently using a glossary.

Remind pupils of the purpose of a glossary: to explain the meaning of words to the reader and of any words or terms that are specific to the subject of the text.

Using some of the key words identified in both the text and these notes, scan the glossary to find some of the meanings. Point out that the words are in alphabetical order rather than subject order.

Pages 47–8

Geography

Key concepts
◆ To use secondary sources.
◆ To use ICT to access information.

Literacy

Use these pages to teach the pupils the purpose and function of a **bibliography** and an index.

Point out to pupils that a bibliography:
◆ collates all the references to other sources made in the text;
◆ provides a reference point for further reading;
◆ is organized alphabetically using the surname of the author;
◆ sometimes provides the ISBN number as well as the title of the reference;
◆ contains some of the following sources: books, websites, articles, periodicals and journals.

Use the bibliography to find further details about one aspect of mountains. Ensure the pupils use a wide range of sources referenced.

Discuss how different source material, e.g. websites, books, are organized. Compare details provided in *Mountains* with material found in a different source.

Point out that an index is organized alphabetically, giving page numbers.

Encourage pupils to practise skimming and scanning text to locate the index word on the page referred to.

Teaching pupils how to read and write recount text

Page 39

written
recount

Reading a recount text

Read p 39 of *Mountains* pupils' book with the pupils. You will need:

◆ the written recount on p 39 (the text-only version on p 21 of these notes can be enlarged/photocopied/made into an OHT for annotation);
◆ p 20 of the notes enlarged/photocopied/made into an OHT for annotation.

SHARED
READING
ACTIVITY

Audience and purpose

Talk about how the intended audience and purpose affects language and layout.

Audience – pupils who may have little or no knowledge of George Mallory.
Purpose – to chronicle the life of George Mallory, focusing particularly on his 1924 expedition to Everest.

SHARED
WRITING
ACTIVITY

Content and organization

Show pupils how the content of this biographical recount is organized by showing it as a skeleton timeline (see p 23 of these notes). Events are organized in chronological order and divided into sections which will make suitable paragraphs.

SHARED
READING
ACTIVITY

Language features and style

Return to the text and talk about the way the language has been used to achieve the effects the author intended (see annotated example on p 22 of these notes).

Note that the text featured is a biography and as such will have certain characteristics:

◆ written in the third person;
◆ factual, concise writing;
◆ retelling the major events in the subject's life in chronological sequence;
◆ containing references to time, date and year.

INDEPENDENT
WRITING
ACTIVITY

Pupils, using their own research, compile a skeleton timeline of another explorer/climber.

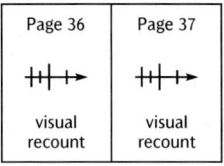

Page 36	Page 37
ᚻᚻᚻ➝	ᚻᚻᚻ➝
visual recount	visual recount

Writing a recount text

Use pp 36–37 of *Mountains* pupils' book as a basis for pupils' own recount texts. You will need:

◆ the visual recount on pp 36–37;
◆ p 20 of these notes enlarged/photocopied/made into an OHT for annotation.

SHARED READING ACTIVITY

Content and organization

Revise the content and organization of the recount text from the previous session (see p 18 of these notes).

INDEPENDENT/ PAIRED READING AND WRITING

In pairs, the pupils read and discuss the visual recount on pp 36–37. Draw the pupils' attention to the chronological sequence of events which led to Hillary's ascent of the Everest.

Explain to the pupils that they are going to rewrite this visual recount as a written recount in the style of the biography of Mallory on p 39 of the pupils' book. In planning their work, the pupils will need to consider the following features (you may wish them to make notes on each feature):

◆ introductory paragraph, describing Hillary's ambition;
◆ clear references to dates and times throughout;
◆ a mention of Hillary's training;
◆ an introduction to Tenzing Norgay;
◆ a chronicle of the ascent;
◆ a mention of Mallory, the Queen, Coronation day.

Pupils may want to make use of the interview with Hillary on p 38 of the pupils' book. It would be beneficial to encourage the pupils to conduct further research into the life of Sir Edmund Hillary – using books, magazines and the Internet – to find out more about his childhood, his family background, any other occupations he may have had.

Language features and style

Remind pupils of the language features of recount texts (see p 20 of these notes).

SHARED WRITING ACTIVITY

Audience and purpose

Discuss the audience for pupils' recounts (readers who may have little or no knowledge of Hillary and his expedition to Everest) and the purpose (to introduce Hillary and to chronicle the events which led to his ascent of Everest).

Once the pupils have assembled enough information about Hillary, show them how to begin the biography, by demonstrating the first paragraph, for example,

From an early age, Edmund Hillary wanted to be a mountaineer. He had often dreamed of conquering Everest, the world's highest peak...

Pupils complete the biography of Edmund Hillary.

INDEPENDENT WRITING ACTIVITIES

Pupils write a biography of someone they know or a member of their family.

About recount text

Audience and purpose

Audience – someone who may not know much about the events.

Purpose – to retell events that actually happened (a true story).

> *Sometimes you may know more about the age or interests of your reader*

Content and organization

- **introductory paragraph** sets the scene, so the reader has all the basic facts needed to understand the recount
- **introduction** often hints at the main event of the recount
- events written in **chronological order** – time order
- **closing statement** – sentence(s) or paragraph to bring the recount to an end

> *Use your introductory sentence to help you write your conclusion. If the introduction is a question then answer it in your conclusions*

> *Answer the questions who? what? when? where?*

> *First this happened … then this happened … next …*

Language features

- written in the **past tense** because these are specific events that only happened once
- focus on **specific people, places, dates**, etc.
- may be written in the **first** or **third person**
- words and devices to show **time order**

> *Stick to one or the other – don't mix them up*

> *This usually means proper nouns, so remember the capital letters!*

> *First…, next…, finally…, In 1950…, Some weeks later…*

The basic skeleton for making notes is a timeline

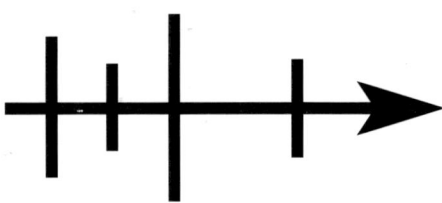

An example of a recount text

George Leigh Mallory was born in 1886. Mallory was a school master but during the First World War he served at the front as a gunner. He was married with three children.

In 1924 a British expedition set out to climb Everest. At that time, no climber had been above 8000 m. It wasn't clear whether climbers could go higher and still survive, and whether oxygen would help.

George Mallory, then 38 years old, was one of Britain's best rock climbers, and he had already proved his fitness on expeditions to Everest in 1921 and 1922. His companion was a scientist called Andrew 'Sandy' Irvine, aged 22. Sandy had no high-altitude climbing experience. However, he was extremely good at repairing the oxygen bottles. The local Tibetans and Sherpas laughed at the bottles. They said they contained 'English air'.

On the morning of 6 June 1924, Mallory and Irvine had a breakfast of fried tinned sardines and set off from their camp at 7667 m. They planned to reach the summit three days later. On the way, they passed another climber, Howard Somervell, who lent his camera to Mallory so that he could take photographs if he reached the top.

Mallory and Irvine were last seen on 8 June by a geologist, Noel Odell, who was following behind . . .

Language features and style of the recount text

Past tense throughout, e.g. was, served

Detail to interest reader

Specific places mentioned

Writing organized in paragraphs, each paragraph outlining a particular aspect of the recount

Discrete reference to dates set in historical context

Written in the third person

Specific people referred to

George Leigh Mallory was born in 1886. Mallory was a school master but during the First World War he served at the front as a gunner. He was married with three children.

In 1924 a British expedition set out to climb Everest. At that time, no climber had been above 8000 m. It wasn't clear whether climbers could go higher and still survive, and whether oxygen would help.

George Mallory, then 38 years old, was one of Britain's best rock climbers, and he had already proved his fitness on expeditions to Everest in 1921 and 1922. His companion was a scientist called Andrew 'Sandy' Irvine, aged 22. Sandy had no high-altitude climbing experience. However, he was extremely good at repairing the oxygen bottles. The local Tibetans and Sherpas laughed at the bottles. They said they contained 'English air'.

On the morning of 6 June 1924, Mallory and Irvine had a breakfast of fried tinned sardines and set off from their camp at 7667 m. They planned to reach the summit three days later. On the way, they passed another climber, Howard Somervell, who lent his camera to Mallory so that he could take photographs if he reached the top.

Mallory and Irvine were last seen on 8 June by a geologist, Noel Odell, who was following behind ...

If you are using this text with other year groups then also highlight these features:

Y3/P4
◆ Distinguishing between first and third person forms of pronouns.
◆ Writing a first person account (e.g. excerpt from Mallory's diary).

Y4/P5
◆ Writing newspaper style reports (e.g. reporting the expedition and how Mallory and Irvine are missing).
◆ Making short notes, e.g. by abbreviating ideas, selecting key words, listing or in diagrammatic form.

Y5/P6
◆ Identifying the features of recount texts, including introductory paragraph, chronological sequence, supporting illustrations and degree of formality adopted.

Content and organization of the recount text

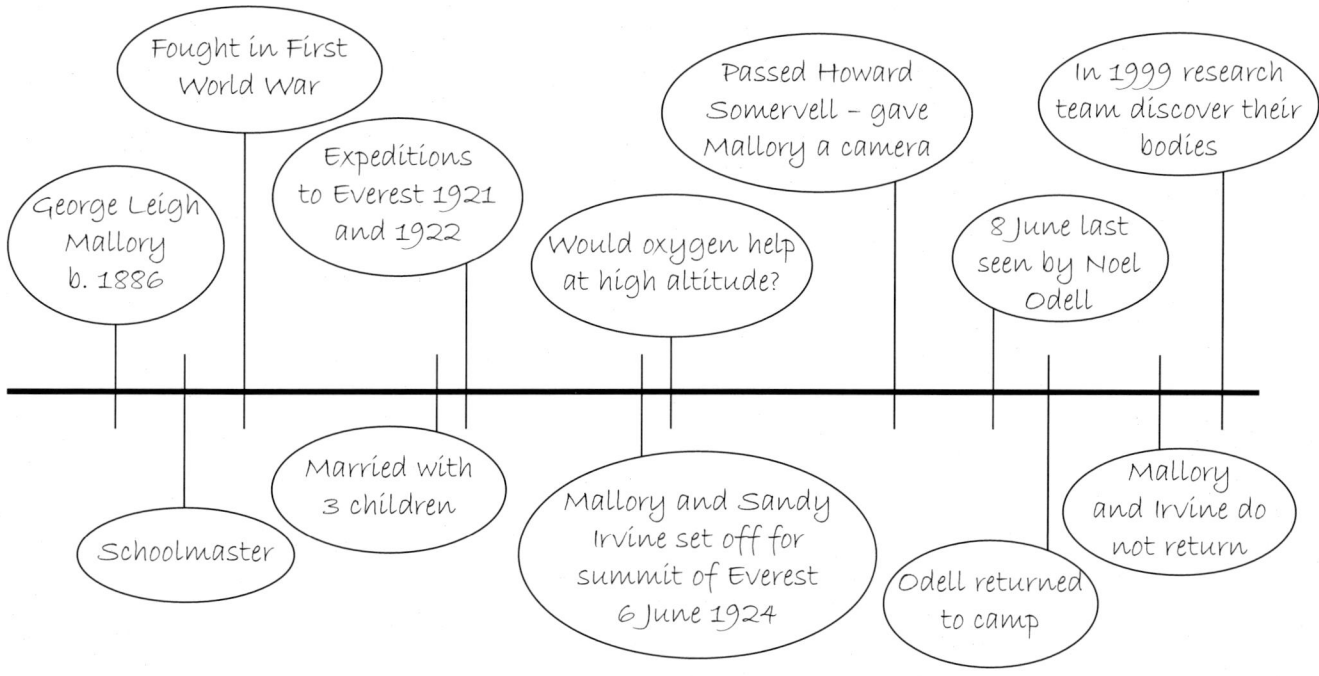

Teaching pupils how to read and write in journalistic style (recount)

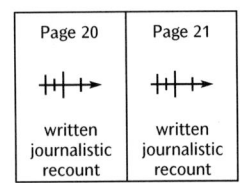

Page 20	Page 21
┼┼┼→	┼┼┼→
written journalistic recount	written journalistic recount

Reading a text written in journalistic style

Read pp 20–21 of *Mountains* pupils' book with the pupils. You will need:

- the text on pp 20–21 (the text-only version on p 27 of these notes can be enlarged/photocopied/made into an OHT for annotation);
- p 26 of these notes enlarged/photocopied/made into an OHT for annotation.

SHARED READING ACTIVITY

Audience and purpose

Define journalistic style – a report or recount of events that provides commentary and opinion.

Talk about how the intended audience and purpose affects language and layout.

Audience – readers of the newspaper who may not have yet heard anything about this particular news item.

Purpose – to inform readers of the events in this news item, how the men became lost, how they survived and were rescued.

SHARED WRITING ACTIVITY

Content and organization

Show pupils how the content of this text is organized by presenting it as a recount skeleton text (see p 29 of these notes). Events are organized in chronological order and divided into sections which will make suitable paragraphs. Highlight that in this journalistic recount there is an introduction of background information, then the chronological order of events.

SHARED READING

Language features and style

Return to the text and talk about how the language has been used to achieve the effects the author intended (see annotated version on p 28). Note useful features for later use in pupils' own writing, e.g. quotes (*They dug into a drift on the mountain ...*); how detail is added to interest the reader (*Each time they climbed out to make a telephone call the temperature inside dropped terribly ...*).

Make particular reference to:

- the use of headlines, subheadings and accompanying illustrations to attract reader's attention;
- use of different font sizes, bold type and italics;
- use of columns to enable the reader to read quickly.

INDEPENDENT ACTIVITY

Ask the pupils to work in groups to discuss the different ways information has been presented in the newspaper report and the diary entries. Which has the most impact?

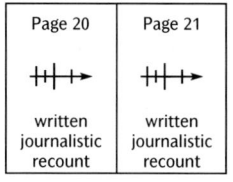

Page 20	Page 21
written journalistic recount	written journalistic recount

Writing a text using journalistic style

Use the visual recount entitled *Landslides* on pages 20–21 of *Mountains* pupils' book as a basis for the pupils' own journalistic style texts. You will need:

◆ the visual recount on pp 20–21;
◆ p 26 of these notes enlarged/photocopied/made into an OHT for annotation.

SHARED READING ACTIVITY

Content and organization

Revise the content and organization of the journalistic style text from the previous session (see p 24 of these notes).

SHARED READING AND WRITING ACTIVITY

In pairs, pupils read and discuss the visual recount on pp 20–21. Draw the pupils' attention to the chronological sequence of events.

Explain to the pupils that they are going to rewrite the visual recount as a written recount in the journalistic style of the text entitled *Three Men Survive Blizzard*. In planning their work, the pupils will need to consider the following components:

◆ eye-catching headline and subheadings;
◆ accompanying illustrations and captions;
◆ reporter's name;
◆ reported speech;
◆ a sharp, exciting opening paragraph;
◆ further paragraphs to divide the story into a chronological sequence;
◆ a lively and concluding paragraph to round off the story.

Ask pupils to make notes on each feature.

Language features and style

Remind pupils of the language features of journalistic texts (see p 26 of these notes).

Audience and purpose

Discuss the audience for the pupils' recount (readers who were not present when the landslides struck and would like to find out what happened) and the purpose (to recount the events which took place in the Kumaon Hills during 11–18 August 1998).

SHARED WRITING ACTIVITY

Once the pupils have planned their work, share some ideas for relevant headlines in class and demonstrate the opening paragraphs for them, e.g:

LANDSLIDE CAUSES DEVASTATION IN HIMALAYAS

'Whole villages have been erased – it's the worst natural disaster I've been involved in,' commented one rescue worker.

Forty-one people have died and thirty-nine remain missing in a major landslide in India. Rocks and mud began cascading down mountain slopes in the Kumaon Hills on Tuesday. Rivers burst their banks as a wall of mud, rock and water barrelled down the gorge . . .

INDEPENDENT WRITING ACTIVITY

Pupils complete the recount independently.

About journalistic style recount

Audience and purpose

Audience – readers who want to know about events that have taken place when they weren't there.

Purpose – to inform readers of events and to influence reader's thoughts by taking an angle and providing bias and opinion.

Content and organization

◆ generally uses either a **report** or **recount** structure depending on the details of events and the angle taken
◆ either tells events as they happened (recount) or as they are (report)
◆ provides a **headline** summarizing the story, a subheading giving a little more detail, **leading sentences** which summarize details such as who? when? what? etc.
◆ often provides a **commentary** on the events and the present situation

Language features

◆ **past** or **present tense** depending on the text structure (report or recount)
◆ use of **sensational/exaggerated** language for effect
◆ **impersonal tense** or **passive** voice to create sense of distance and impartiality on the part of the writer
◆ **reported speech** (*Joe Smith, the director, commented that…*)
◆ use of speech to quote key players' comments

The basic skeleton for making notes is a timeline

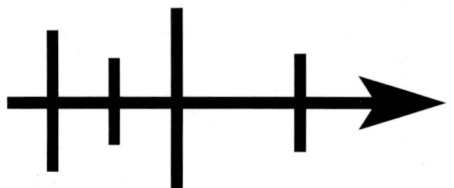

An example of a journalistic style text

Three Men Survive Blizzard

"They dug into a drift on the mountain and closed the hole behind them. It was like a marmot's den."

By Paul Webster

Three Alpine skiers who spent nine nights at 3000 metres in blizzards and sub-zero temperatures were recovering in hospital yesterday after a rescue operation that combined raw courage, ingenuity and high technology. A week after they lost their way in a blizzard while trekking across peaks in the Savoie, France, the three were saved after France Telecoms pinpointed a call on their portable telephone. The rescue team leader said the 'excellent' survival techniques used by the three men, who built an igloo inside a 10-metre-high snowdrift, should be used as an example for all mountaineers.

The men set off for a four-day trek on Monday 15 February. Five days after they had set off, the men made their first call to rescuers. They could give no accurate information on where they were holed up.

The leader of the mountain rescue team, Gerard Valich, a police captain, said:

"They called again twice on Sunday but the battery ran out before the call could be traced."

Language features and style of the journalistic style text

Three Men Survive Blizzard

"They dug into a drift on the mountain and closed the hole behind them. It was like a marmot's den."

By Paul Webster

Three Alpine skiers who spent nine nights at 3000 metres in blizzards and sub-zero temperatures were recovering in hospital yesterday after a rescue operation that combined raw courage, ingenuity and high technology. A week after they lost their way in a blizzard while trekking across peaks in the Savoie, France, the three were saved after France Telecoms pinpointed a call on their portable telephone. The rescue team leader said the 'excellent' survival techniques used by the three men, who built an igloo inside a 10-metre-high snowdrift, should be used as an example for all mountaineers.

The men set off for a four-day trek on Monday 15 February. Five days after they had set off, the men made their first call to rescuers. They could give no accurate information on where they were holed up.

The leader of the mountain rescue team, Gerard Valich, a police captain, said:

"They called again twice on Sunday but the battery ran out before the call could be traced."

Eyecatching heading, followed by leading quote to set the scene

First paragraph summarizes events

Use of sensational, descriptive language for effect

Use of past tense verbs

Use of reported speech

Reference to dates to show sequence of events

Connectives that signal time

Use of direct speech

Quotation from key player

If you are using this text with other year groups then also highlight these features:

Y3/P4
- Investigating through reading and writing how words and phrases can signal time sequences, e.g. *after, then, before, when.*
- Experimenting with recounting the same event in a variety of ways, e.g. in the form of a story, a letter, a news report.

Y4/P5
- Identifying the main features of newspapers, including lay-out, range of information, voice, level of formality; organization of articles and headlines.
- Predicting newspaper stories from the evidence of headlines.

Y5/P6
- Using connectives to link clauses within sentences and to link sentences in longer texts.
- Identifying the features of recounted texts including: introduction to orientate reader; chronological sequence; degree of formality adopted.

Content and organization of the journalistic style text

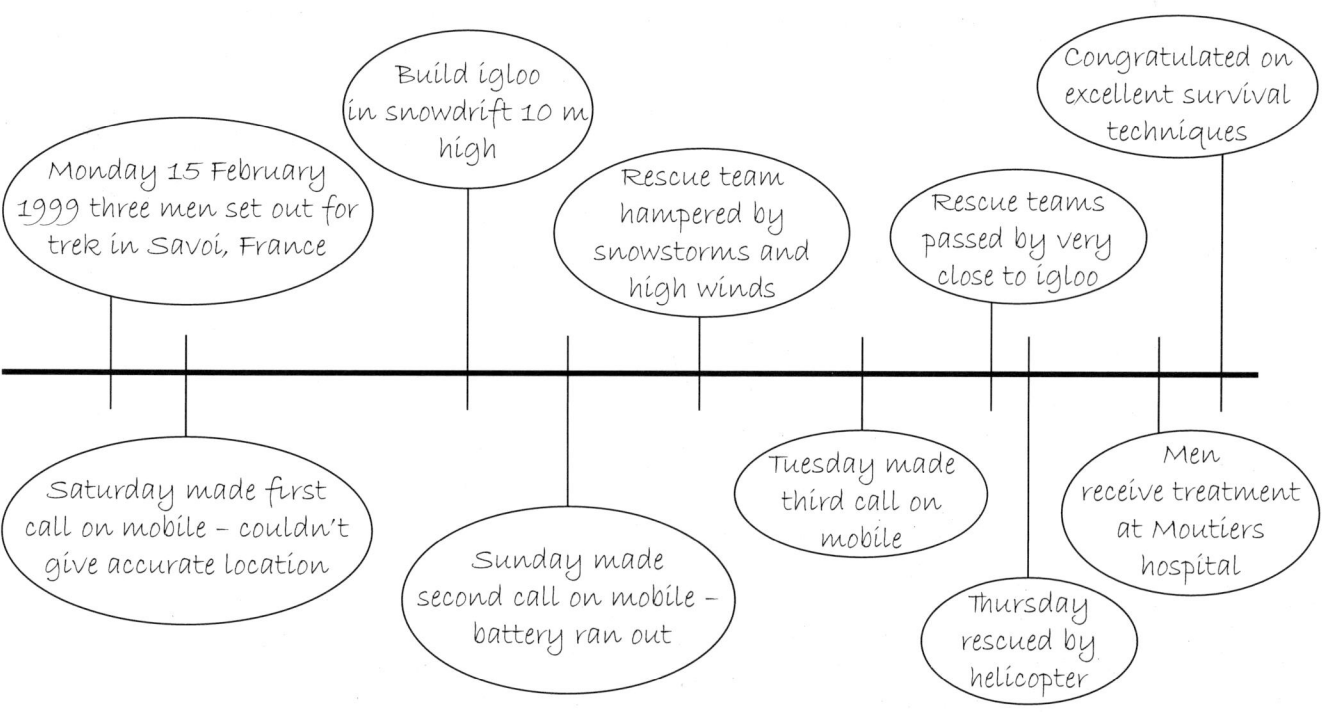

Teaching pupils how to read and write report text

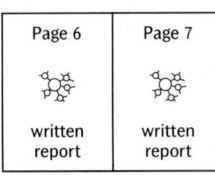

Page 6	Page 7
written report	written report

Reading a report text

Read pp 6–7 of *Mountains* pupils' book with the pupils. You will need:

◆ the report text on pp 6–7 (the text-only version on p 33 of these notes can be enlarged/photocopied/made into an OHT for annotation);
◆ p 32 of these notes enlarged/photocopied/made into an OHT for annotation.

> SHARED
> READING
> ACTIVITY

Audience and purpose

Talk about how the intended audience and purpose affects language and layout.

Audience – pupils who want to learn more about the lives of people who live in mountainous areas.

Purpose – to provide information about the Sherpas of Nepal, the hill tribes of Mount Kinabalu and the Andean people.

> SHARED
> WRITING
> ACTIVITY

Content and organization

Show pupils how the content of this non-chronological report text is organized by showing its content in a report skeleton (see p 35 of these notes). Each paragraph becomes one arm of the report skeleton and details are noted around it.

> SHARED
> READING
> ACTIVITY

Language features and style

Return to the text and talk about the way language has been used to achieve the effects the author intended (see annotated version on p 34 of these notes). Make particular reference to: the use of the present tense throughout; the use of the third person narrative throughout; the use of concise, factual sentences, avoiding descriptive/emotional language; information presented in non-chronological order.

> INDEPENDENT
> ACTIVITY

Pupils use the information on one of the hill tribes to prepare a television documentary-style report.

Writing a report text

Use pp 24–25 of *Mountains* pupils' book as a basis for pupils' own report texts.
You will need:

◆ the visual report on pp 24–25;
◆ p 32 of these notes enlarged/photocopied/made into an OHT for annotation.

> SHARED READING ACTIVITY

Content and organization

Revise the content and organization of the report text from the previous session (see p 30 of these notes).

> PAIRED READING AND WRITING ACTIVITY

In pairs, pupils read and discuss the visual report on pp 24–25 of the pupils' book and discuss how sections of the report skeleton notes may be formed into paragraphs. They should consider carefully the order of the paragraphs and if any additional information needs to be included, e.g. detail from the photographs.

Language features and style

Remind pupils of the language features of reports (see p 32 of these notes).

> SHARED WRITING ACTIVITY

Audience and purpose

Discuss the audience for the pupils' reports (readers who would like to know more about mountain industries) and the purpose (to describe the range of industries which exist in mountainous regions and to highlight their dependence on the mountain climate).

Demonstrate writing a short introductory paragraph, e.g.:

Many people depend upon the natural resources and climate of mountainous regions for work and food.

The climate in such areas of high altitude supports industries from traditional farming and crafts, to mining, energy production, forestry and tourism.

The heavy rainfall in some mountain regions enables local farmers to grow a range of saleable crops including rice, tea, potatoes and strawberries.

> INDEPENDENT WRITING ACTIVITY

Pupils complete the report independently.

About report text

Audience and purpose

Audience – someone who wants to know about the topic.
Purpose – to describe what something is like.

Sometimes you may know more about the age or interests of your reader

Content and organization

- **non-chronological** information
- **introductory sentence or paragraph** says what the report is going to be about
- the information is sorted into groups or **categories**
- reports may include short pieces of explanation

This means it ISN'T written in time order, like a story or recount

What something looks like, where it is found . . .

Language features

- written in the **present tense**
- usually **general nouns and pronouns** (not particular people or things)
- **factual descriptive words**, not like the descriptions in a story
- words and devices that show **comparison and contrast**
- **third person** writing to make the report **impersonal and formal**
- **technical words and phrases** – which you may need to explain to the reader
- use of **examples** to help the reader understand the technical words

You would write about dogs in general, not a particular dog

You would say powerful beams, not beautiful bright beams

Expressions like have in common, the same as . . ., on the other hand, however . . .

Unusual words that go with the topic such as canine, translucent and wing span

Wingspan is the distance between the tips of a bird's outstretched wings

The basic skeleton for making notes is a spidergram

An example of a report text

Mountain people

A tenth of the world's total population lives in the mountains. Mountains are home to several thousand different tribes or ethnic groups.

The Sherpas of Nepal.

The word 'Sherpa' means 'people of the east'. Sherpa people originally came from eastern Tibet, but from about 1400 AD onwards, this mountain tribe began to migrate, and today about 36,000 Sherpas live in the Himalayas, in Nepal. No one on Earth lives at a higher altitude than the Sherpas.

The Sherpas are very well equipped for mountain living. They have lived for centuries at high altitude, and so their lungs have developed more fully than those of people who live at lower altitudes. Therefore, they are able to pump oxygen into their bloodstream and muscles much more efficiently than many other people. This, combined with the fact that they are generally small and stocky, helps them to tolerate low temperatures, and enables them to climb very high mountains. As a result they have acquired an international reputation as first class mountain guides. When, in 1953, Sir Edmund Hillary made the first successful attempt at climbing Mount Everest, his guide was a Sherpa called Tenzing Norgay.

Language features and style of the report text

- Present tense throughout, e.g. *are*
- General nouns throughout, e.g. *people*
- Style formal, factual
- Third person
- Non-chronological

Mountain people

Introductory paragraph to orientate reader and set the topic for the report —

A tenth of the world's total population lives in the mountains. Mountains are home to several thousand different tribes or ethnic groups.

Subheading — **The Sherpas of Nepal**

The word 'Sherpa' means 'people of the east'. — *Technical term, 'Sherpa' defined*

Sherpa people originally came from eastern Tibet, but from about 1400 AD onwards, this mountain tribe began to migrate, and today about 36,000 Sherpas live in the Himalayas, in Nepal. No one on Earth lives at a higher altitude than the Sherpas. — *Information about origins of Sherpas*

Use of the present tense — The Sherpas are very well equipped for mountain living. They have lived for centuries at high altitude, and so their lungs have developed more fully than those of people who live at lower

Information about Sherpas now — altitudes. Therefore, they are able to pump oxygen into their bloodstream and muscles much more — *General nouns*

efficiently than many other people. This, combined with the fact that they are generally — *A complex sentence, with multiple clauses to give as many facts as possible in a concise way*

Factual adjectives — small and stocky, helps them to tolerate low temperatures, and enables them to climb very high mountains. As a result they have acquired an international reputation as first class mountain

Example to back up point — guides. When, in 1953, Sir Edmund Hillary made the first successful attempt at climbing Mount Everest, his guide was a Sherpa called Tenzing Norgay. — *Phrase to signal consequence*

If you are using this text with other year groups then also highlight these features:

Y3/P4 ◆ Writing simple non-chronological reports from known information, using notes made to organize and present ideas.

Y4/P5 ◆ Writing a non-chronological report, including the use of organizational devices.

Y5/P6 ◆ Planning, composing and editing short non-chronological reports – pupils to write a similar report, introducing themselves and their families.

Content and organization of the report text

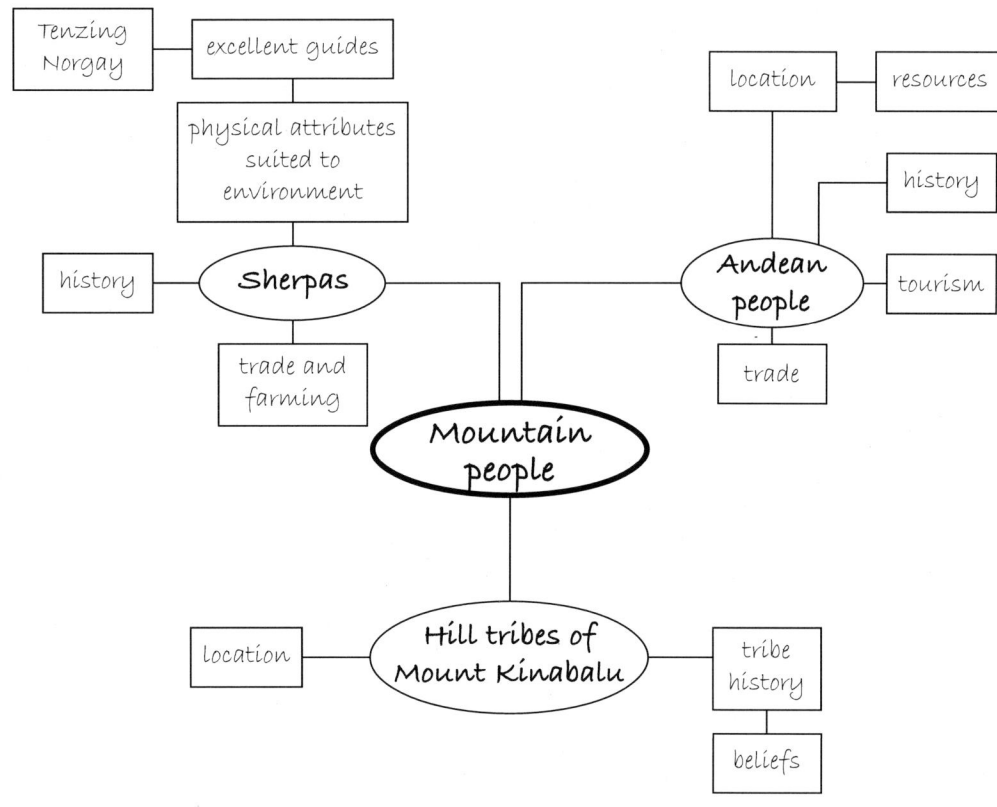

Teaching pupils how to read and write explanation text

Page 14

written explanation

Reading an explanation text

Read p 14 of *Mountains* pupils' book with the pupils. You will need:

◆ the written explanation on p 14 (the text-only version on p 39 of these notes can be enlarged/photocopied/made into an OHT for annotation);
◆ p 38 of these notes enlarged/photocopied/made into an OHT for annotation.

> SHARED
> READING
> ACTIVITY

Audience and purpose

Talk about how the intended audience and purpose affects language and layout.

Audience – readers who wish to understand how a fold mountain is formed.
Purpose – to explain how fold mountains are formed.

> SHARED
> WRITING
> ACTIVITY

Content and organization

Show pupils how the content of this explanation text is organized by showing it in a skeleton flowchart (see p 41 of these notes).

> SHARED
> READING
> ACTIVITY

Language features and style

Return to the text and talk about the way language has been used to achieve the effects the author intended (see annotated version on p 40 of these notes). Draw attention to the use of technical vocabulary, e.g. *plates, mantle*, etc. Discuss how it is sometimes effective to use diagrams to support the information in the written text.

> INDEPENDENT
> ACTIVITY

Pairs of pupils with the use of props (for example two pieces of card), describe to an audience the formation of fold mountains using the information supplied in the explanation text.

Page 14	Page 15
♀⚭♀	♀⚭♀
written explanation	visual explanation

Writing an explanation text

Use pp 14–15 of *Mountains* pupils' book as a basis for the pupils' own explanation texts. You will need:

◆ the visual explanation on p 15;
◆ p 38 of these notes enlarged/photocopied/made into an OHT for annotation.

Content and organization

SHARED
READING
ACTIVITY

Revise the content and organization of the explanation text from the previous session (see p 36 of these notes).

INDEPENDENT/
PAIRED READING
AND WRITING

The pupils, working in pairs or individually, discuss the visual explanation entitled *How a volcano is formed* and make skeleton notes in preparation for rewriting the text as a written explanation, in the style of *Fold mountains*.

For the pupils to write effective explanations, they will first need to understand the process for themselves. It would be a good idea for them to conduct further research into how volcanoes are formed – using books, encyclopaedias and Internet sites – so that their written explanations are detailed and well-informed.

Their notes will form the basic plan for their written texts and may look like this:

◆ begin with definition of terms – *volcano, magma, Earth's crust*;
◆ explanation of magma lying underneath the Earth's crust;
◆ explanation of the movement of plates colliding;
◆ description of how and why the magma moves upwards towards the surface;
◆ final description of how the volcano is formed as a result.

Language features and style

Remind pupils of the language features of explanation texts (see p 38 of these notes).

SHARED
WRITING
ACTIVITY

Audience and purpose

Discuss the audience for the pupils' explanation texts (readers who know little or nothing about how volcanoes are formed) and the purpose (to explain clearly how volcanoes are formed).

Check that the pupils have understood the process of how a volcano is formed, through class discussion and diagrams on the board.

Demonstrate how to write the written explanation by beginning the first paragraph for the pupils, for example:

A volcano is a 'vent' in the Earth's crust through which molten rock material, or magma and gases can erupt to the surface. Within the rock or mantle below the Earth's crust there are chambers of molten rock called magma…

Explain to the pupils that the next paragraph will explain about the Earth's plates, e.g.:

The Earth's crust is divided up into plates. These plates are continually moving and colliding. Where two plates collide…

PAIRED
WRITING
ACTIVITY

Ask pupils in pairs to complete the paragraph.

Pupils continue the explanation, writing the next two paragraphs, e.g.

INDEPENDENT
WRITING
ACTIVITY

The pressure created by the submerging plate forces the magma to find its way up through cracks in the Earth's crust …

Magma and gases find their way to the surface and a volcanic eruption occurs. Magma cools to form lava. The distinctive shape of a volcano is determined by the type of material expelled by the volcano. Thick lava will form tall volcanoes. Runny lava will form flatter volcanoes.

About explanation text

Audience and purpose

Audience – someone who wants to understand the process (how or why it happens).

Purpose – to explain how or why something happens.

> Sometimes you may know more about the age or interests of your reader

Content and organization

- **title** often asks a question, or says clearly what the explanation is about
- text often opens with **general statement(s)** to introduce important words or ideas
- the process is then written in a **series of logical steps**, usually in **time order**
- sometimes picture(s) or diagram(s)

> This happens... then this happens... next...

Language features

- **third person** writing to make the explanation **impersonal and formal**
- written in the **present tense**
- usually **general nouns and pronouns** (not particular people or things)
- **factual descriptive words**, not like the descriptions in a story
- **technical words and phrases** – which you may need to explain to the reader
- words and devices that show **sequence**
- words and devices that show **cause and effect**

> You would say powerful beams, not beautiful bright beams

> You would write about dogs in general, not a particular dog

> Unusual words that go with the topic such as, canine, translucent and wingspan

> First..., next..., finally

> If..., then... This happens because... This means that...

The basic skeleton for making notes is a flowchart

> The explanation skeleton can change depending on the sort of process

An example of an explanation text

Fold mountains

The Earth's crust is divided into large sections called plates. The plates are huge chunks of rock that float on the top of the soft mantle of the Earth. Geologists believe that the Earth's plates are constantly moving at a speed of about 1–10 cm a year. Sometimes two plates crash into each other. When they collide, they create intense pressure, causing the plates to buckle. This causes rock to be pushed upwards, forming a mountain. Imagine taking a piece of paper and putting it flat on your desk. If you pushed the two ends towards each other, you would get an upward fold in the middle. That's what can happen when the Earth's plates collide with each other.

A good example of a chain of fold mountains is the Himalayas. They were created 25 million years ago because the Indian plate collided with the Eurasian plate. An older chain of fold mountains is the Urals. They are approximately 200 million years old.

Language features and style of the explanation text

Fold mountains

The Earth's crust is divided into large sections called plates. The plates are huge chunks of rock that float on the top of the soft mantle of the Earth. Geologists believe that the Earth's plates are constantly moving at a speed of about 1–10 cm a year. Sometimes two plates crash into each other. When they collide, they create intense pressure, causing the plates to buckle. This causes rock to be pushed upwards, forming a mountain. Imagine taking a piece of paper and putting it flat on your desk. If you pushed the two ends towards each other, you would get an upward fold in the middle. That's what can happen when the Earth's plates collide with each other.

A good example of a chain of fold mountains is the Himalayas. They were created 25 million years ago because the Indian plate collided with the Eurasian plate. An older chain of fold mountains is the Urals. They are approximately 200 million years old.

Technical vocabulary explained in following sentence

Present tense verbs

Description of collision

Useful analogy to simplify difficult concept

Words and phrases to show cause and effect

Examples to clarify explanation

If you are using this text with other year groups then also highlight these features:

Y3/P4 ◆ Locating information, using contents, index, headings, subheadings (e.g. research topic on volcanoes).

Y4/P5 ◆ Using sub-headings, paragraphs and connectives to improve the cohesion of written explanations.
◆ Identifying the features of explanatory texts including: purpose, structure and language features – see 'About explanation text', p 38 in these notes.

Y5/P6 ◆ Reading a range of explanatory texts, investigating and noting features of impersonal style, e.g. complex sentences; passive voice; hypothetical language (if, then, might . . .), causal connectives.
◆ Conveying power, reflections or moods in poetry – using the theme of volcanoes to write their own compositions.

Content and organization of the explanation text

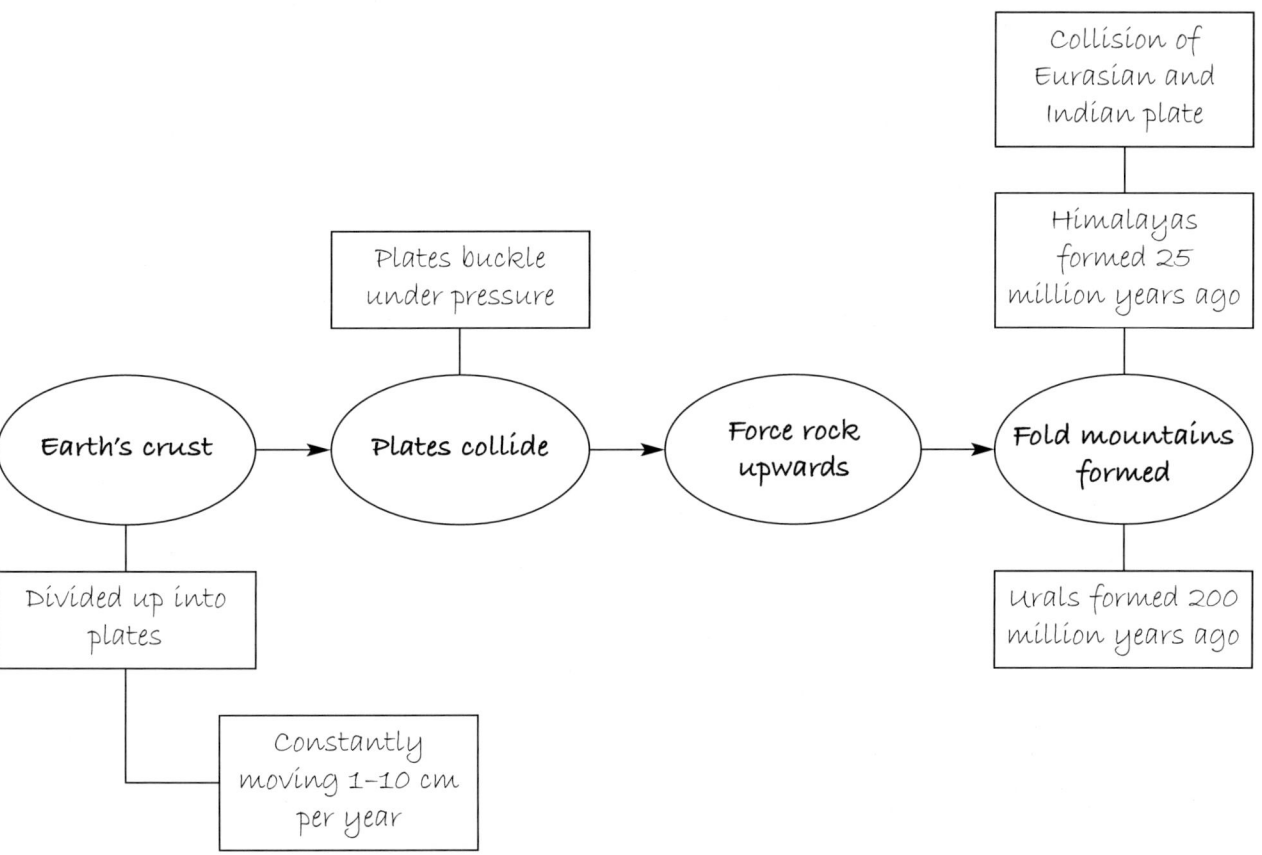

Teaching pupils how to read and write discussion text

Reading a discussion text

Page 26	Page 27
| **|** **|** **|** **|** **|** written disscussion	**|** **|** **|** **|** **|** **|** written disscussion

Read pp 26–27 of *Mountains* pupils' book with the pupils. You will need:

◆ the discussion text on pp 26–27 (the text-only version on p 45 of these notes can be enlarged/photocopied/made into an OHT for annotation);
◆ p 44 of these notes enlarged/photocopied/made into an OHT for annotation.

> SHARED
> READING
> ACTIVITY

Audience and purpose

Define discussion text – a text that presents differing viewpoints of an issue. Talk about how the intended audience and purpose affects the language and layout.

Audience – pupils wishing to know more about the arguments for and against cutting down trees.

Purpose – to present arguments and information from different viewpoints on the subject of deforestation.

> SHARED
> WRITING
> ACTIVITY

Content and organization

Show pupils how the content of this discussion text is organized by presenting it as a skeleton text (see p 47 of these notes). Identify the basic structure of the discussion argument and counter argument. Point out:

◆ sentences that introduce arguments, then elaborate upon them with detailed evidence, e.g. paragraph two;
◆ evidence for arguments drawn from other areas already covered.

Identify that each paragraph has evidence to support both arguments and that the first and last paragraphs introduce and conclude the text. Ask pupils to summarize the arguments for and against and the key evidence cited in support of them.

> SHARED
> READING
> ACTIVITY

Language features and style

Return to the text and talk about the way the language has been used to achieve the effects the author intended (see annotated example on p 44 of these notes). Point out:

◆ the title summarizes the key issue;
◆ introductory paragraph to explain the subject of controversy – clearing of the rainforest;
◆ formal language which creates impartiality, e.g. *It is therefore important that mountain communities are maintained*;
◆ deeper analysis of each argument – first dealing with *for* then *against*;
◆ brief summary of both sides of the argument, before studying each viewpoint in more detail;
◆ supporting evidence and examples throughout;
◆ connectives used to signal contrasting viewpoints, e.g. *At the same time . . .*
◆ final summary – including author's own opinion – suggesting compromise (i.e. striking a balance between the short-term needs of the people and the long-term effects on the environment).

> INDEPENDENT
> ACTIVITY

Divide the class into two groups (one half in favour of deforestation, the other not). Ask the pupils to find more evidence in support of their arguments using the pupils' book and other sources to present to the class in a formal debate. Remind the pupils that impartiality and formal language are required.

Deciding on one view point, pupils design posters to put forward their argument.

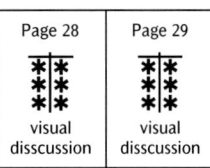
Writing a discussion text

Use pp 28–29 of *Mountains* pupils' book as the basis for the pupils' own writing. You will need:

◆ the visual discussion on pp 28–29;

◆ p 44 of these notes enlarged/photocopied/made into an OHT for annotation.

> SHARED READING ACTIVITY

Content and organization

Revise the content and organization of instruction text from the previous session (see p 42 of these notes).

> INDEPENDENT/ PAIRED READING AND WRITING

Ask pupils to discuss in pairs the visual discussion on pp 28–29 in the pupils' book, making reference to the ways in which this text differs from the written discussion text on pp 26–27 (i.e. this text lists opposing views in the form of quoted speech from local pupils). In changing the visual text into a full written discussion text, the pupils will need to consider the central point at the heart of each of the local pupils' comments, for example:

FOR	AGAINST
beautiful views	lack of entertainment in off peak season
winter sports on your doorstep	a feeling of remoteness
clean and healthy air to breathe	few opportunities for cycling
many interesting pursuits	difficult journeys to school every day
plenty of opportunities to keep fit	long commute to work
rare animals and plants to appreciate	few normal shops for locals
tourism bringing new faces to meet	tourists bring congestion and litter
plenty of part-time work for teenagers	very cold weather conditions in winter
job opportunities in busy tourist season	risk of avalanches

Language features and style

Remind pupils of the language features of discussion texts (see p 44 of these notes).

Audience and purpose

Discuss the audience for pupils' discussion texts (readers who wish to know more about the advantages and disadvantages of living in a mountain resort) and the purpose (to present arguments for and against living in a mountain resort).

> SHARED WRITING ACTIVITY

Ask the pupils to write the visual text as a written discussion text in the style of pp 26–27 of the pupils' book. Demonstrate by writing an introductory paragraph that summarizes the issue, for example:

Many of us may have visited mountains on holiday, but what would it be like to live in such a beautiful place all year round. Idyllic? For some children life in a mountain resort is wonderful, with magnificent views, a healthy life style and plenty of skiing. For others, however, the harsh reality of enduring boring days in isolated mountain villages can be too much to bear …

Demonstrate, using the skeleton notes, how to plan the next paragraphs, going into more detail about the advantages and disadvantages and then drawing a conclusion, using impartial language.

> INDEPENDENT WRITING ACTIVITY

Pupils complete the activity, writing another three paragraphs and a concluding paragraph. Ensure that the conclusion shows a preference for one viewpoint over another.

✳ About discussion text

Audience and purpose

Audience – someone who wants to know both sides of the argument, but may not know much about the subject.

> Sometimes you may know more about the age or interests of your reader.

Purpose – to present arguments and information from different viewpoints.

Content and organization

- usually starts with a sentence or paragraph **introducing the subject** under discussion and **defining important terms**

> Introduce important words or ideas the reader needs to know

- the argument is then split into a number of **main points for and against**

> You can either give all the arguments for, then all the arguments against, or all arguments for and against each point – one by one

- the arguments for and against are supported by **evidence and examples**

> The examples could:
> – agree with the point
> – back up the evidence
> – add further information to explain it

- **concluding sentence or paragraph** sums up the main points, for and against (and sometimes expresses the author's own opinions).

Language features

- written in the **third person** to make the discussion **impersonal and formal**

> Give the people on each side names, such as Supporters claim..., Critics reply...

- usually in the **present tense**
- usually **generalized nouns** (except in specific examples)

> Environ-mentalists, developers, scientists...

- words and devices showing **cause and effect,** used to **argue** the case

> Therefore..., Consequently..., This means that...

- words and devices that signal a **move from one side of the argument** to the other

> However..., On the other hand...

- words and devices which suggest 'possibility' rather than certainty

> Perhaps..., probably..., might..., could be...

The basic skeleton for making notes is a for-and-against grid

✳✳
✳✳✳
✳✳

An example of a discussion text

The future of the mountain forest

Healthy mountain forests are extremely important to the world. They protect the watersheds that supply half the fresh water we use. They are also home to thousands of wild animals and plants. At the same time, the wood that they provide gives many thousands of people a source of money. Should we protect the forests or should we allow them to be cut down?

There are two ways of looking at the future of forests. On the one hand people say that forests are renewable: trees that are cut down can be replaced with new ones. On the other hand, conservationists believe that cutting down forests may have dangerous consequences for all of us.

The people who see forests as a renewable resource argue that we need the wood that forests provide for timber products and paper products. Many poor communities around the world depend on forests for their livelihood. If they are no longer allowed to cut trees down, they will have to find other ways of earning a living . . .

In response to these arguments, conservationists point out that large areas of rainforest and forest are disappearing daily, destroying rare plants and endangering animals. Once these are gone, we can't replace them. Furthermore, as forests are cut down, river beds begin to dry up because there is less rain without the trees . . .

Therefore, it seems that although there are many arguments in favour of cutting down mountain forests, we should think very carefully before allowing a wide-scale logging programme to continue. Perhaps the answer is that we should limit the amount of logging that is allowed each year in an effort to maintain a balance between the immediate needs of the people and the needs of nature.

Language features and style of the discussion text

The future of the mountain forest

Healthy mountain forests are extremely important to the world. They protect the watersheds that supply half the fresh water we use. They are also home to thousands of wild animals and plants. At the same time, the wood that they provide gives many thousands of people a source of money. Should we protect the forests or should we allow them to be cut down?

There are two ways of looking at the future of forests. On the one hand people say that forests are renewable: trees that are cut down can be replaced with new ones. On the other hand, conservationists believe that cutting down forests may have dangerous consequences for all of us.

The people who see forests as a renewable resource argue that we need the wood that forests provide for timber products and paper products. Many poor communities around the world depend on forests for their livelihood. If they are no longer allowed to cut trees down, they will have to find other ways of earning a living . . .

In response to these arguments, conservationists point out that large areas of rainforest and forest are disappearing daily, destroying rare plants and endangering animals. Once these are gone, we can't replace them. Furthermore, as forests are cut down, river beds begin to dry up because there is less rain without the trees . . .

Therefore, it seems that although there are many arguments in favour of cutting down mountain forests, we should think very carefully before allowing a wide-scale logging programme to continue. Perhaps the answer is that we should limit the amount of logging that is allowed each year in an effort to maintain a balance between the immediate needs of the people and the needs of nature.

If you are using this text with other year groups then also highlight these features:

Y4/P5
◆ Reading, comparing and evaluating arguments and discussions, e.g. on the environment.
◆ Assembling and sequencing points of view.
◆ Presenting a point of view in writing.

Y5/P6
◆ Constructing an argument in note form or full text to persuade others of a point of view.

Content and organization of the discussion text

For deforestation	Against deforestation
◆ Logging income for local communities	◆ Habitats destroyed – animals become extinct
◆ Without income people move to cities	◆ Species of plants destroyed
◆ Villages abandoned, culture lost	◆ Affects climate – less rain with fewer trees
◆ World needs wood products	◆ Increases risk of disasters – floods, landslides, avalanches

Conclusion	
Restrict logging but make sure enough to sustain local communities and to meet world needs	Programme of planting trees and protecting endangered animals and plants

Page	Contents	Text Type	National Literacy Strategy Objectives	QCA Geography Objectives Unit 15
	Concept map Contains	Reference		*Pupils should learn:*
4	Landscapes and mountains	Visual report	T1 TL 12, 13, 17 T1 SL 2, 3, 4, 5, 6 T1 WL 6 T2 TL 10, 11, 12	• about different types of environments and specifically a mountain one • about the world distribution of major mountain areas • to use globes and atlases • how the environment affects the nature of human activity
6	Mountain people	Written report	T1 TL 12,13, 17 T1 SL 2, 3, 4, 5, 6 T1 WL 2, 3, 6	
8	Where are the mountains?	Visual report	T1 TL 12, 13, 17 T1 SL 2, 3, 4, 5, 6 T1 WL 6	
10	Why do mountains matter?	Written explanation	T1 TL 17 T3 TL 15, 19 T3 SL 1, 3, 4	
12	Some mountain ranges	Visual report	T1 TL 12, 13, 17 T1 SL 2, 3, 4, 5, 6 T1 WL 6	• to investigate how mountain environments are similar and different in nature across a range of places and scales • to use secondary sources
14	Peaks and domes	Written and Visual explanation	T1 TL 9, 10 T2 TL 3, 5, 6 T3 TL 15, 19 T3 SL 1, 3, 4	
16	Under the volcano	Written explanation Visual instruction	T1 TL 12,13 T1 SL 2, 3, 4, 5, 6 T1 WL 6	
18	The Mountain climate	Visual report	T1 TL 12, 13, 17 T1 SL 2, 3, 4, 5, 6 T1 WL 2, 3, 6	• about weather patterns in different parts of the world • that varying weather conditions can have a significant impact on life in an area • to use secondary sources
20	Severe weather warnings	Written and Visual recount	T1 TL 15, 16 T1 SL 2, 3, 4, 5, 6 T1 WL 2, 3, 6, 8	
23	Weather reports	Visual report	T1 TL 12,13 T1 SL 2, 3, 4, 5, 6 T1 WL 2, 3, 6	
24	Working in the mountains	Visual report	T1 TL 12, 13, 17 T1 SL 2, 3, 4, 5, 6 T1 WL 6	• about different types of environment and specifically a mountain one • how the environment affects the nature of human activity
26	The future of the mountain forest	Written discussion	T2 15, 16, 18, 19 T2 SL 1, 3, 4, 5 T2 WL 5, 8	• how the environment affects the nature of human activity
28	Mountain life	Visual discussion	T2 TL 15, 16, 18, 19 T2 SL 1, 3, 5 T2 WL 2, 3, 8	
30	Let's go to the mountains!	Written and Visual persuasion	T1 TL 15, 17 T1 SL 5	
32	Postcards from high places Sponsored mountain walk	Written recount Written report Written persuasion	T1 TL 15, 16 T1 SL 2, 3, 4, 5, 6 T1 WL 6, 8	
34	Mountain safety	Written instruction	T1 TL 11, 12 T1 SL	
36	The ascent of Everest	Visual recount (biography)	T1 11, 14 T1 SL 2, 3, 4, 5, 6 T1 WL 2, 3, 6	• about different types of environment and specifically a mountain one • to use secondary sources
38	Mountain experts	Written discussion Written recount (biography)	T1 TL 11, 14 T1 SL 2, 3, 4, 5, 6 T1 WL 2, 3, 6, 8	
40	Tourism in the mountains – good or bad?	Visual discussion	T2 TL 15, 16, 18, 19 T2 SL 1, 3, 5 T2 WL 2, 3, 8	• that the effect of tourism can be significant in a given area and can be both good and bad • to use secondary sources
42	Mountain manners	Visual persuasion	T2 15, 16, 18, 19 T2 SL 1, 3, 4, 5 T2 WL 5, 8	• that the effect of tourism can be significant in a given area and can be both good and bad
44	Saving the mountain environment	Visual discussion	T2 TL 15, 16, 18, 19 T2 SL 1, 3, 5 T2 WL 2, 3, 8	• that the effect of tourism can be significant in a given area and can be both good and bad • to use secondary sources
46	Glossary	Reference		• about different types of environment and specifically a mountain one
47	Bibliography	Reference		• to use secondary sources • to use ICT to access information
48	Index	Reference		